An Educational Coloring Book

of

# ENDANGERED SPECIES

**EDITOR**
Linda Spizzirri

**ASST. EDITOR**
Jacqueline Sontheimer

**ILLUSTRATION**
Peter M. Spizzirri

**COVER ART**
Peter M. Spizzirri

# CONTENTS

An Educational Coloring Book of ENDANGERED SPECIES • Published by SPIZZIRRI PUBLISHING, INC., P.O. BOX 9397, RAPID CITY, SOUTH DAKOTA 57709. No part of this publication may be reproduced by any means without the express written consent of the publisher. All national and international rights reserved on the entire contents of this publication.
Printed in U.S.A.

| | |
|---|---|
| NAME: | HAWAIIAN MONK SEAL (*Monachus schauinslandi*) |
| HOW MANY ARE LIVING TODAY: | 1,000 to 1,500 |
| WHERE IT LIVED: | ALL OF THE HAWAIIAN ISLANDS |
| WHERE IT LIVES TODAY: | WESTERN MOST HAWAIIAN ISLANDS |
| WHAT IT EATS: | REEF FISH AND MOLLUSKS |
| COLOR IT: | UPPER PARTS GRAYISH WITH DARK SPOTS, UNDER PARTS YELLOWISH-WHITE |
| INTERESTING FACTS: | Christopher Columbus found Carribean monk seals on his first voyage to the new world. Today these Carribean and the Florida monk seals are extinct. |

The Hawaiian monk seal is the only surviving tropical pinniped of the United States. Although the Hawaiian monk seal appears tame, it seems incapable of tolerating human presence. If any human appears where they are living and birthing their young, they will move and not return to that area.

| | |
|---|---|
| NAME: | CALIFORNIA CONDOR (*Gymnogyps californianus*) |
| HOW MANY ARE LIVING TODAY: | NO MORE THAN 60 |
| WHERE IT LIVED: | WEST OF THE ROCKY MOUNTAINS FROM CANADA TO CALIFORNIA |
| WHERE IT LIVES TODAY: | MOUNTAINS NORTHWEST OF LOS ANGELES ONLY |
| WHAT IT EATS: | CARRION ONLY MAKING IT HARMLESS AND BENEFICIAL |
| COLOR IT: | DARK GRAY-BROWN FEATHERS WITH WHITE EDGES ON INNER WINGS, LIGHT RED HEAD, GRAY BEAK, PALE PINK LEGS AND FEET |
| INTERESTING FACTS: | This large member of the vulture family has a wing span of 9 to 9½ feet and is a strong soaring bird. Its large feet are made for standing and walking, not grasping. It will, however, roost on large dead trees. This beneficial bird is almost extinct because we've altered its habitat, disturbed its nesting areas and killed many believing it was a menace to livestock. Population growth is doubtful because each female lays only one egg every second year. |

| | |
|---|---|
| **NAME:** | AMERICAN ALLIGATOR (*Alligator mississippensis*) |
| **HOW MANY ARE LIVING TODAY:** | UNKNOWN |
| **WHERE IT LIVED:** | ONCE COMMON IN SOUTHEASTERN SWAMPS OF UNITED STATES |
| **WHERE IT LIVES TODAY:** | SWAMPS IN FLORIDA, MISSISSIPPI AND LOUISIANA |
| **WHAT IT EATS:** | FISH, TURTLES, CRABS, BIRDS, ANY ANIMAL AT THE WATER'S EDGE OR OTHER ALLIGATORS |
| **COLOR IT:** | GRAY-GREEN ABOVE, YELLOWISH-WHITE BELOW |
| **INTERESTING FACTS:** | Most of an alligator's time is spent basking lazily in the sun close to the water's edge. The female lays her eggs on shore in a nest of plant debris which serves as a natural incubator, and relies on the warm sun to hatch them. Alligators prefer fresh water, and unlike the crocodile, will not swim in salt water. Both alligators and crocodiles were hunted to near extinction because there was a great demand for their skins. Today both are protected by law. |

| | |
|---|---|
| NAME: | MOUNTAIN LION, COUGAR, PUMA (*Felis concolor*) |
| HOW MANY ARE LIVING TODAY: | UNKNOWN |
| WHERE IT LIVED: | ALL OF CANADA, UNITED STATES, MEXICO AND SOUTH AMERICA |
| WHERE IT LIVES TODAY: | 12 WESTERN STATES AND FLORIDA IN THE UNITED STATES |
| WHAT IT EATS: | OTHER ANIMALS, DEER AND ELK |
| COLOR IT: | YELLOW-BROWN ABOVE, WHITISH BELOW |
| INTERESTING FACTS: | The mountain lion is the largest cat in North America. Because of its attacks on domestic livestock, there have been persistent efforts to kill all mountain lions. In many cases federal and state agencies have aided in the execution by offering bounties. Today, America's only lion lives exclusively in the wildest areas of the country. |

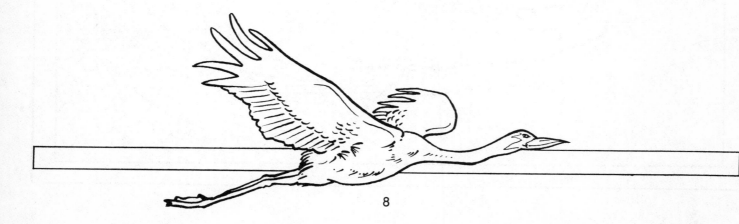

| | |
|---|---|
| NAME: | KEY DEER (*Odocoileus virginianus clavium*) |
| HOW MANY ARE LIVING TODAY: | INCREASED FROM ONLY 50 DEER 20 YEARS AGO TO 350 DEER TODAY |
| WHERE IT LIVED: | FLORIDA KEYS |
| WHERE IT LIVES TODAY: | FLORIDA KEYS |
| WHAT IT EATS: | MANGROVE LEAVES AND OTHER PLANTS BECAUSE OF ITS UNUSUAL TOLERANCE FOR SALT |
| COLOR IT: | BLACK NOSE, WHITE LOWER LIP, GRAYISH-BROWN UPPER BODY, GRAY-WHITE BELLY AND INSIDE LEGS |
| INTERESTING FACTS: | The key deer is a powerful swimmer, capable of crossing channels between the islets of the Florida Keys. This tiny deer, which is no larger than an Irish setter, was almost extinct by 1960. Today, it is protected as an endangered species, but large herd growth does not seem possible. Two reasons for this are the automobile accidents involving the deer and the lack of fresh water available during the dry season. |

| | |
|---|---|
| NAME: | WHOOPING CRANE (*Grus americana*) |
| HOW MANY ARE LIVING TODAY: | LESS THAN 100 |
| WHERE IT LIVED: | BREEDING: NORTHERN MIDWEST STATES, ALASKA & CANADA WINTERED: TEXAS AND LOUISIANA ALONG THE GULF OF MEXICO |
| WHERE IT LIVES TODAY: | BREEDING: WOOD BUFFALO NAT. PARK IN CANADA WINTER: ARANSAS WILD LIFE REFUGE IN TEXAS |
| WHAT IT EATS: | INSECTS, EARTH WORMS, BIRDS, EGGS, FISH, GRAIN & GRASS SHOOTS |
| COLOR IT: | WHITE WITH BLACK WING TIPS AND BLACK FACE MASK, GRAY LEGS, A RED HEAD PATCH |
| INTERESTING FACTS: | The whooping crane was so named because of its peculiar whooplike call that can be heard for 2 miles. It is the tallest of all American birds at 5 feet tall, and is one of the rarest. Planned conservation refuges may have come too late. Any further population increase of this beautiful bird will be directly related to the amount of habitat available. Cranes will not mate without an undisturbed marsh area of 1,000 acres per pair. |

| | |
|---|---|
| NAME: | RED WOLF (*Canis rufus*) |
| HOW MANY ARE LIVING TODAY: | ABOUT 24 |
| WHERE IT LIVED: | SOUTHEASTERN UNITED STATES FROM CENTRAL TEXAS TO PENN-SYLVANIA |
| WHERE IT LIVES TODAY: | A BREEDING FACILITY IN TACOMA, WASHINGTON |
| WHAT IT EATS: | RABBITS AND SMALL RODENTS |
| COLOR IT: | OVERALL RED-BROWN, BLACK HAIR ON BACK, TAIL AND TIP OF TAIL, GRAYISH RED FACE, WHITE CHIN AND NECK |
| INTERESTING FACTS: | The red wolf resembles the gray wolf but it is smaller in size and has shorter fur. Human persecution caused a steady elimination of the red wolf because we did not understand that its diet consisted only of rabbits and small rodents. By 1970 the only red wolf population left was in a small area of southwest Louisiana and southeastern Texas. The U.S. Fish and Wildlife Service captured and evacuated the wolves to Tacoma, Washington with the hope of saving these beneficial animals from extinction. |

| | |
|---|---|
| NAME: | MEXICAN GRIZZLY BEAR (*Ursus arctos*) |
| HOW MANY ARE LIVING TODAY: | A FEW SURVIVORS WERE FOUND IN 1969 |
| WHERE IT LIVED: | MEXICO. ONLY ARIZONA AND NEW MEXICO IN THE UNITED STATES |
| WHERE IT LIVES TODAY: | IN THE YAQUI BASIN OF SONORA |
| WHAT IT EATS: | OTHER ANIMALS, BIRDS, INSECTS, ROOTS, BERRIES AND FISH |
| COLOR IT: | LIGHT BROWN FACE AND BACK, DARK BROWN BELLY, LEGS AND FEET |
| INTERESTING FACTS: | The Mexican grizzly bear is a type of brown bear. They got the name grizzly bear from the light colored hairs that grow at the tip of their thick brown fur coats making them look "grizzled." In North America they are among our largest meat eating mammals. After being hunted, trapped and poisoned these animals are now under formal protection by Presidential proclamation. |

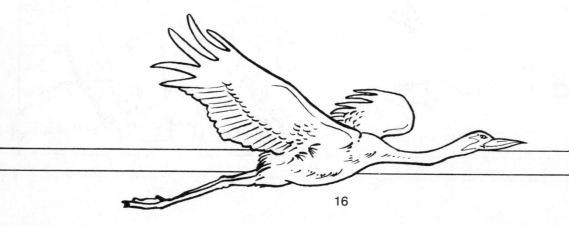

| | |
|---|---|
| NAME: | WALRUSES (*Odobenus rosmarus*) |
| HOW MANY ARE LIVING TODAY: | 45,000 to 75,000 |
| WHERE IT LIVED: | FROM ARCTIC OCEAN SOUTH TO THE WESTERN SHORES OF OREGON |
| WHERE IT LIVES TODAY: | ARCTIC OCEAN TO THE NORTHWEST COAST OF ALASKA |
| WHAT IT EATS: | CLAMS, MOLLUSKS AND OTHER MARINE LIFE |
| COLOR IT: | OVER ALL REDDISH-BROWN WITH WHITE TUSKS |
| INTERESTING FACTS: | The ancestors of walruses can be traced back 15 million years. At that time they were abundant in Arctic waters around the world.<br>The Eskimo uses every part of the walrus for food, boats, shelter, oil and charms. Many hunters kill walruses strictly for their tusks and they kill them in great numbers. Because the female walrus gives birth to only one pup every two years, if this hunting continues the walruses will disappear. |

NAME: EASTERN BROWN PELICAN
(*Pelecanus occidentalis*)

HOW MANY ARE
LIVING TODAY: UNKNOWN

WHERE IT LIVED: FROM EASTERN MEXICO AROUND THE GULF STATES ALONG THE ATLANTIC OCEAN TO N. CAROLINA

WHERE IT LIVES
TODAY: FLORIDA EVERGLADES ONLY

WHAT IT EATS: FISH ONLY

COLOR IT: DARK BROWN WITH A WHITE STRIPE ON ITS NECK AND A YELLOW FOREHEAD

INTERESTING FACTS: The brown pelican is the smallest of all pelicans and is the only plunge-diving pelican in the world. Pelicans lay their eggs at the same nesting site every year, but will not lay eggs at the same site if the water around it has been polluted. Brown pelicans no longer breed in Louisiana possibly due to the contamination of the Mississippi River.

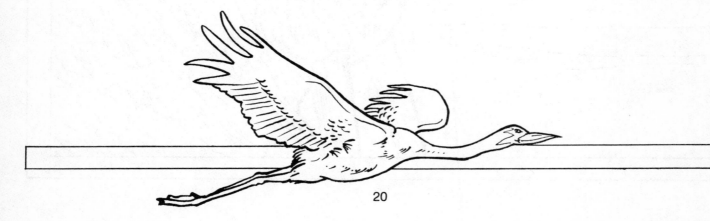

| | |
|---|---|
| NAME: | BLACK-FOOTED FERRET (*Mustela nigripes*) |
| HOW MANY ARE LIVING TODAY: | UNKNOWN |
| WHERE IT LIVED: | GRASSLANDS OF NORTH AMERICA FROM CANADA TO TEXAS |
| WHERE IT LIVES TODAY: | UNKNOWN |
| WHAT IT EATS: | PRAIRIE DOGS, MICE, GOPHERS AND GROUND SQUIRRELS |
| COLOR IT: | LIGHT TAN UPPER PARTS, BLACK MASK, LEGS AND TIP OF TAIL |
| INTERESTING FACTS: | The constant war on prairie dogs, the chief prey of the black-footed ferret, has resulted in the near extinction of this beneficial animal. Sightings of the ferret are rare because it hunts mostly underground in the passageways of prairie dog burrows and because it is mainly active at night and at dawn. Daylight hours are spent in the abandoned burrows of its prey. |

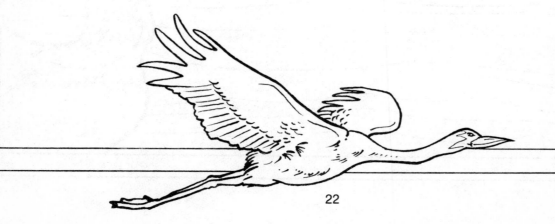

| | |
|---|---|
| NAME: | PRONGHORN (*Antilocapra americana*) |
| HOW MANY ARE LIVING TODAY: | INCREASED FROM 15,000 IN 1910 to 500,000 TODAY |
| WHERE IT LIVED: | ALL STATES WEST OF ILLINOIS FROM CANADA TO MEXICO |
| WHERE IT LIVES TODAY: | IN THE ROCKY MOUNTAINS WITH THE GREATEST NUMBERS IN STATES OF MONTANA AND WYOMING |
| WHAT IT EATS: | SHRUBS, GRASSES, WEEDS AND OTHER VEGETATION |
| COLOR IT: | UPPER PARTS RED-BROWN TO TAN, WHITE BANDS ON NECK, WHITE RUMP AND UNDERPARTS |
| INTERESTING FACTS: | The pronghorn is the fastest mammal in America, capable of speeds up to 65 miles an hour. Before the arrival of settlers, they roamed the western half of the United States by the millions. The population and range of the pronghorn was reduced, by man, to near extinction. Efforts to save the species were successful and proved that conservation practices can work, if they are applied. |

| | |
|---|---|
| **NAME:** | WOOD BISON, AMERICAN BUFFALO<br>(*Bison bison athabascae*) |
| **HOW MANY ARE LIVING TODAY:** | 200 FOUND IN 1957 |
| **WHERE IT LIVED:** | MOST OF WESTERN NORTH AMERICA |
| **WHERE IT LIVES TODAY:** | WOOD BUFFALO NATIONAL PARK IN CANADA |
| **WHAT IT EATS:** | LEAVES, SHRUBS, GRASS AND TWIGS |
| **COLOR IT:** | REDDISH-BROWN BODY WITH DARK BROWN FACE, LEGS AND FEET AND GRAYISH-BROWN HORNS. YOUNG ARE COMPLETELY RED-BROWN |
| **INTERESTING FACTS:** | It is estimated, that at one time, more than 60 million bison lived in North America. It is the heaviest of America's land animals, weighing one ton or more. By 1900 the government outlawed all bison hunting and set aside land for its protection.<br>It was thought that the wood bison had completely integrated with the plains bison and was extinct, but in 1957, 200 were found in the most remote part of Canada's Wood Buffalo National Park. |

| NAME: | IVORY-BILLED WOODPECKER<br>(*Campephilus principalis*) |
| HOW MANY ARE LIVING TODAY: | UNKNOWN (In 1952 a pair and nestling were sighted in Florida) |
| WHERE IT LIVED: | IN THE SWAMPLANDS OF SOUTH-EASTERN AND CENTRAL UNITED STATES |
| WHERE IT LIVES TODAY: | FLORIDA |
| WHAT IT EATS: | INSECTS AND SPIDERS |
| COLOR IT: | OVERALL BLACK WITH RED CREST ON HEAD, WHITE STRIPES ON NECK AND BODY, WHITE END FEATHERS ON WINGS |
| INTERESTING FACTS: | The ivory-billed woodpecker is the largest (20 inches long) woodpecker in the United States. It is one of America's rarest birds. The National Audubon Society established a 1,300 acre sanctuary in the Apalachicola River country of Florida after the 1952 sighting. This was done in the hope that there would be more birds in the area. |

Since each mating pair of ivory-bills require about two thousand acres of uncut forest for their territory, it has little chance of population growth and may already be extinct.

| | |
|---|---|
| NAME: | SWIFT FOX (*Vulpes macrotis*) |
| HOW MANY ARE LIVING TODAY: | UNKNOWN |
| WHERE IT LIVED: | SOUTHWESTERN CANADA TO TEXAS |
| WHERE IT LIVES TODAY: | SOUTHWESTERN CANADA TO TEXAS |
| WHAT IT EATS: | RABBITS, LIZARDS, RODENTS, BIRDS, INSECTS AND VEGETATION |
| COLOR IT: | GRAY-BROWN UPPER PARTS, RED-BROWN SIDES, FLANKS & LEGS WITH WHITE BELLY AND INNER LEGS, BLACK NOSE AND TIP OF TAIL |
| INTERESTING FACTS: | The shy swift fox are night hunters, who spend the daylight hours sleeping in their burrows. They take one mate for life and are excellent parents, sharing in the care and training of their young. Alteration of their habitat and being hunted for their valuable fur are reasons why they are near extinction. Poisoned baits have been very successful in killing entire families. They are now protected in some states as an endangered species. |

# Educational Coloring Books and
# STORY CASSETTES

The only non-fiction coloring book/cassette packages available! The cassettes are not read-alongs. Rather, the educational factual information in the coloring book is utilized and enhanced to create exciting stories. Sound, music, and professional narration stimulate interest and promote reading. Children can color and listen, color alone, or simply listen to the cassette. We are proud to offer these quality products at a reasonable price.

**DISPLAY RACKS AVAILABLE. INDIVIDUALLY PACKAGED.**

## YOUR CHOICE OF 48 TITLES

"ISBN (INTERNATIONAL STANDARD BOOK NUMBER) PREFIX ON ALL BOOKS AND CASSETTES: 0-86545-

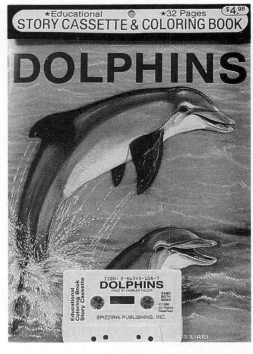

★Educational — ★32 Pages — $4.98
STORY CASSETTE & COLORING BOOK
DOLPHINS

| | | |
|---|---|---|
| No. 082-X | DINOSAURS | |
| No. 083-8 | Prehistoric SEA LIFE | |
| No. 084-6 | Prehistoric BIRDS | |
| No. 085-4 | CAVE MAN | |
| No. 086-2 | Prehistoric FISH | |
| No. 087-0 | Prehistoric MAMMALS | |
| No. 097-8 | Count/Color DINOSAURS | |
| No. 089-7 | PLAINS INDIANS | |
| No. 090-0 | NORTHEAST INDIANS | |
| No. 091-9 | NORTHWEST INDIANS | |
| NO. 092-7 | SOUTHEAST INDIANS | |
| No. 093-5 | SOUTHWEST INDIANS | |
| No. 094-3 | CALIFORNIA INDIANS | |
| No. 153-2 | ESKIMOS | |
| No. 152-4 | COWBOYS | |
| No. 150-8 | COLONIES | |
| No. 151-6 | PIONEERS | |
| No. 154-0 | FARM ANIMALS | |
| No. 095-1 | DOLLS | |
| No. 096-X | ANIMAL ALPHABET | |
| No. 160-5 | CATS | |

| | |
|---|---|
| No. 161-3 | DOGS |
| No. 162-1 | HORSES |
| No. 159-1 | BIRDS |
| No. 147-8 | PENGUINS |
| No. 098-6 | STATE BIRDS |
| No. 163-X | STATE FLOWERS |
| No. 100-1 | MAMMALS |
| No. 101-X | REPTILES |
| No. 158-3 | POISONOUS SNAKES |
| No. 102-8 | CATS OF THE WILD |
| No. 103-6 | ENDANGERED SPECIES |
| No. 157-5 | PRIMATES |
| No. 104-4 | ANIMAL GIANTS |
| No. 148-6 | ATLANTIC FISH |
| No. 149-4 | PACIFIC FISH |
| No. 105-2 | SHARKS |
| No. 106-0 | WHALES |
| No. 107-9 | DEEP-SEA FISH |
| No. 108-7 | DOLPHINS |
| No. 109-5 | AIRCRAFT |
| No. 110-9 | SPACE CRAFT |

| | |
|---|---|
| No. 111-7 | SPACE EXPLORERS |
| No. 112-5 | PLANETS |
| No. 113-3 | COMETS |
| No. 114-1 | ROCKETS |
| No. 155-9 | TRANSPORTATION |
| No. 156-7 | SHIPS |

ALL BOOK CASSETTE PACKAGES $4.98 EACH

---

## LISTEN AND COLOR
## LIBRARY ALBUMS

**6** Educational Coloring Books
Book/Story Cassettes
In a plastic storage case

We have gathered cassettes and books of related subject matter into individual library albums. Each album will provide a new, in-depth, and lasting learning experience. They are presented in a beautiful binder that will store and protect your collection for years.
**We also invite you to pick 6 titles of your chosing and create your own CUSTOM ALBUM.**

LIBRARY ALBUMS $34.95 EACH

---

## CHOOSE ANY LIBRARY ALBUM LISTED, OR SELECT TITLES FOR YOUR CUSTOM ALBUM

| **No. 088-9 Prehistoric Life** | **No. 116-8 American Indian** | **No. 164-8 Oceans & Seas** | **No. 117-6 Air & Space** | **No. 165-6 Americana** |
|---|---|---|---|---|
| Dinosaurs | Plains Indians | Atlantic Fish | Aircraft | Colonies |
| Prehistoric Sea Life | Northeast Indians | Pacific Fish | Space Craft | Cowboys |
| Prehistoric Fish | Northwest Indians | Sharks | Space Explorers | Pioneers |
| Prehistoric Birds | Southeast Indians | Whales | Planets | State Flowers |
| Prehistoric Mammals | Southwest Indians | Deep-Sea Fish | Comets | State Birds |
| Cave Man | California Indians | Dolphins | Rockets | Endangered Species |

| **No. 166-4 Animal Libr #1** | **No. 167-2 Animal Libr. #2** | **No. 168-0 Young Students** | **No. 170-2 New Titles Library** | **No. 169-9 Custom Library** |
|---|---|---|---|---|
| Poisonous Snakes | Prehistoric Mammals | Animal Alphabet | Eskimos | WE INVITE YOU TO PICK 6 TITLES OF YOUR CHOSING AND CREATE YOUR OWN CUSTOM LIBRARY. |
| Reptiles | Birds | Counting & Coloring Dinosaurs | State Flowers | |
| Animal Giants | Farm Animals | Dolls | Penguins | |
| Mammals | Endangered Species | Dogs | Atlantic Fish | |
| Cats of the Wild | Animal Alphabet | Cats | Pacific Fish | |
| Primates | State Birds | Horses | Farm Animals | |